# Teaching Tips

## Encouraging Topic Interest

Help students to develop an understanding of and appreciation for different health concepts. Engage students through stories, non-fiction, easy-to-read books, videos, posters, and other resources as a springboard for learning.

## Black Line Masters and Graphic Organizers

Encourage students to use the black line masters and graphic organizers to present information and reinforce important concepts, and to extend opportunities for learning. The graphic organizers will help students focus on important ideas or make direct comparisons.

## Feelings Face Cards

Use the feelings face cards as a tool to help students identify the way they feel in various situations.

## Learning Logs

Keeping a learning log is an effective way for students to organize their thoughts and ideas about the health concepts presented. Student learning logs also give the teacher insight into which follow-up activities are needed to review and clarify concepts learned.

Learning logs can include the following kinds of entries:

- Teacher prompts
- Student personal reflections
- Questions that arise
- Connections discovered
- Labeled diagrams and pictures

## Rubrics and Checklists

Use the rubrics and checklists in this book to assess student learning.

## Table of Contents

# My Name Is

My name is ___________________________________

1. I am ______________ years old

2. My favorite thing to do is ___________________________________

3. My favorite color is ___________________________________

4. I am special because ___________________________________

# How I Have Changed

| | | When I Was Little | Now |
|---|---|---|---|
| 1. | My size | | |
| 2. | The food I eat | | |
| 3. | The toys I like to play with | | |
| 4. | Where I sleep | | |

# Changes in Your Life

In the chart below, identify a change in your life.
An example might be moving to another place or getting a new pet.

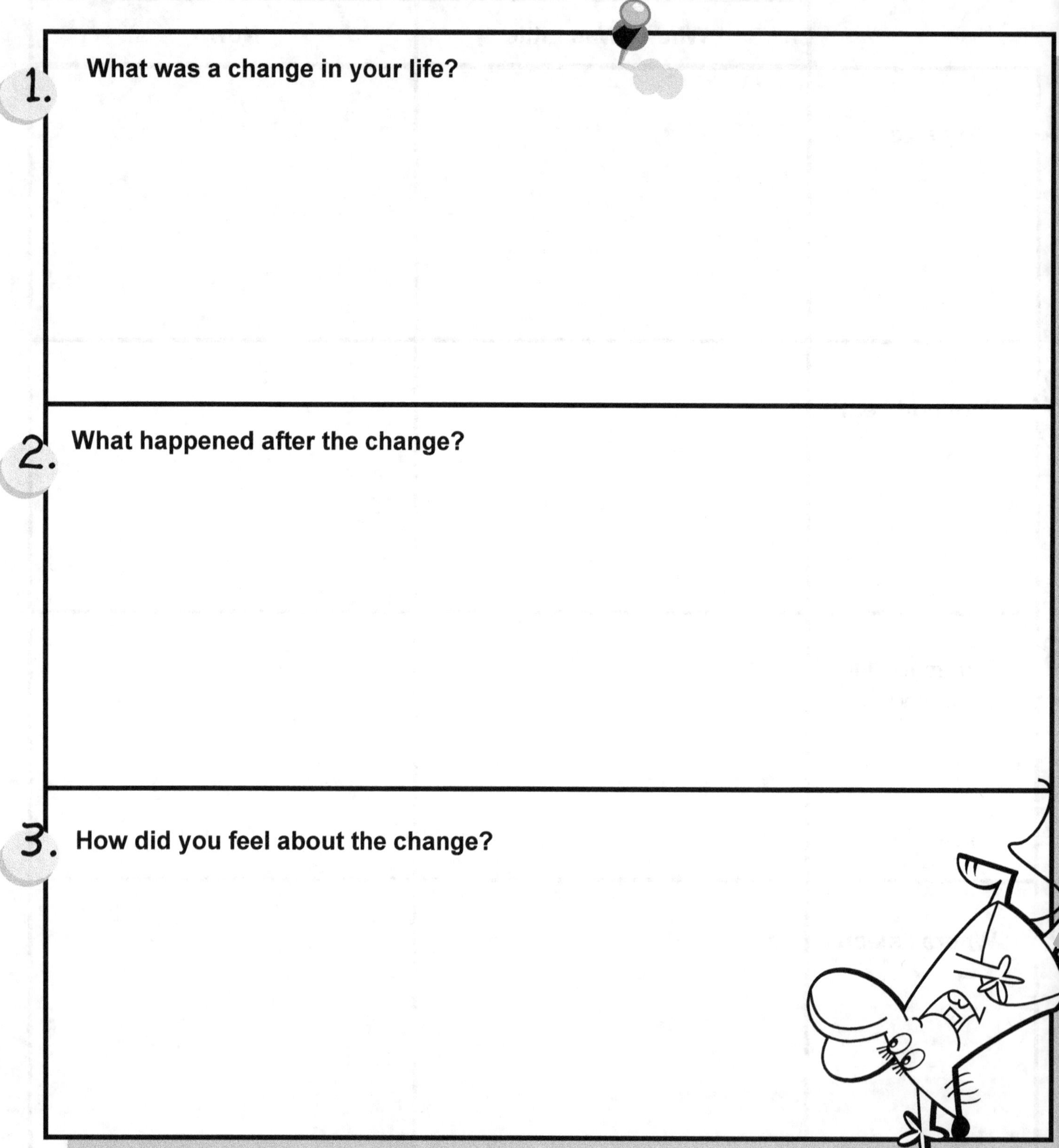

**1.** What was a change in your life?

**2.** What happened after the change?

**3.** How did you feel about the change?

# A Timeline

Create a timeline to show the important events in your life.

| Age | Important Event |
|-----|-----------------|
|     |                 |
|     |                 |
|     |                 |
|     |                 |
|     |                 |
|     |                 |
|     |                 |
|     |                 |

# When I Grow Up

**1.** When I grow up I want to be _______________________________________

**2.** The reason is _______________________________________

_______________________________________

_______________________________________

# Someone Special

**1.** **This is a picture of someone special in my life.**

**2.** ___________________________ **is special to me because...**

________________________________________________

________________________________________________

# Happy Face

1. This is a picture of a happy face.

# Sad Face

1. **This is a picture of a sad face.**

# Angry Face

1. This is a picture of an angry face.

# Scared Face

1. This is a picture of a scared face.

# Worried Face

1. **This is a picture of a worried face.**

# How Would You Feel?

| Situation | I would feel... |
|---|---|
| 1. My friend invited me to their birthday party. | |
| 2. My pet hamster died. | |
| 3. I am moving to another town. | |
| 4. I had a good day. | |
| 5. I had to stay in after school. | |
| 6. Someone bullied me at school. | |
| 7. My friend told me a funny joke. | |
| 8. I had to try something for the first time. | |

# My Feelings

# My Feelings

# All About Friends

1.  What is a friend? _______________________________________

_______________________________________________________

2.  Name a friend from school. _______________________________

3.  Draw a picture of something you and your friend like to do together.

4.  Write about your picture. _________________________________

_______________________________________________________

_______________________________________________________

# All About Friends

**1.** Who is your best friend? _______________________________

**2.** Draw a picture of something you like to do together.

**3.** Write about your picture. _______________________________

_______________________________

_______________________________

**4.** Why is this person your best friend? _______________________________

_______________________________

# How to Be a Friend

1. Pretend there is a new student in class. What would you do to make this new person comfortable in their new class?

_______________________________________________

_______________________________________________

_______________________________________________

_______________________________________________

_______________________________________________

2. Draw a picture of something you can do together.

# Be a Friend T-shirt

Create a T-shirt with a message that shows a tip on how to be a good friend.

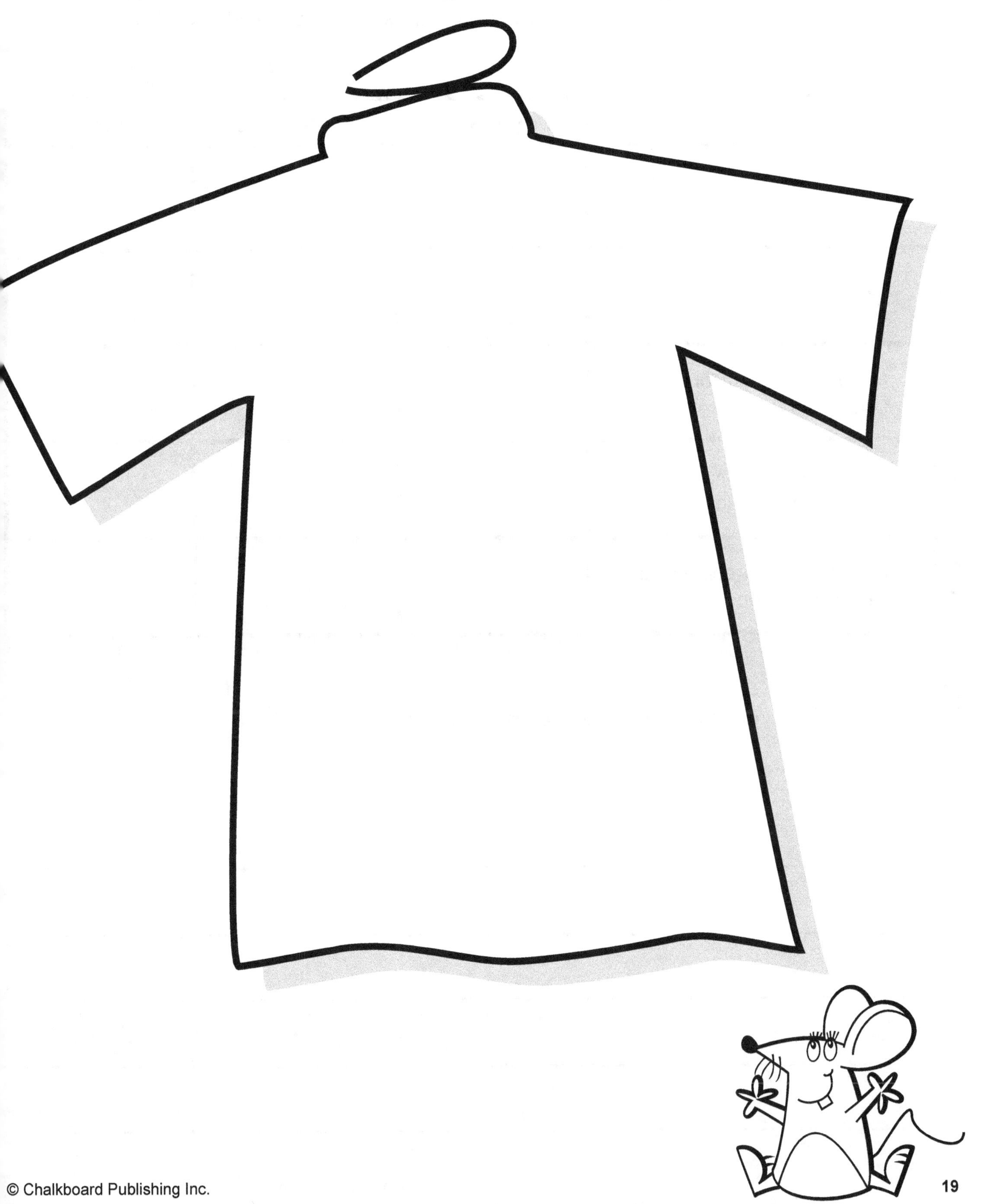

# Cooperation Survey

People get along better when they cooperate with each other.
Here are some ways that people can cooperate with each other.
Take the survey and think about how well you cooperate with others.

| Situation | Always | Sometimes | Never |
|---|---|---|---|
| 1. I share things with others. | | | |
| 2. I take turns. | | | |
| 3. I take responsibility for my share of group work. | | | |
| 4. I tell people when they are doing something well. | | | |
| 5. I talk about disagreements and look for a solution. | | | |

**6.** **Do you think you are a cooperative person? Explain your thinking.**

_____________________________________________________________

_____________________________________________________________

_____________________________________________________________

_____________________________________________________________

_____________________________________________________________

# Likenesses and Differences

Everyone has likenesses and differences.

| | QUESTION | YOUR NAME | YOUR PARTNER'S NAME |
|---|---|---|---|
| 1. | What is your hair color? | | |
| 2. | What is your favorite color? | | |
| 3. | Who is your teacher? | | |
| 4. | Do you have a pet? | | |
| 5. | What is your favorite activity at school? | | |
| 6. | What month were you born in? | | |
| 7. | How are you different? | | |
| 8. | How are you alike? | | |

# Family: Activity Ideas

## Activity Idea: What Is a Family?

In a whole-group setting, brainstorm with students about what makes up a family. Families may be traditional nuclear families, extended families, single-parent families, blended families, foster families, or same-sex-parent families. On a web graphic organizer, outline your family, showing how you are in the middle with different family members around you. Explain your relationship to each family member. For example:

- My mother is my family because I am her daughter/son.
- My brother is my family because we share the same parents/father and/or mother.

The teacher may wish to showcase a different student's family each day. Invite families to send in pictures and to complete questions about their family life and favorite memories.

## Activity Idea: Family Tree

Show students how families differ in size and makeup by creating individual family trees.

1. First, model for students how to trace their hand onto green construction paper and how to carefully cut it out.

2. Have students then cut out a hand for each member of their family.

3. Next, have students write a family member's name on each hand shape. Each hand shape with a family member's name on it will represent a leaf on their family tree.

4. On a piece of paper have students use brown crayon to draw the trunk of their family tree.

5. Demonstrate for students how to place and glue their family member leaves onto their tree trunk.

### Discussion Starters:

- How are the family trees the same or different?

## Activity Idea: Class Graphing Ideas

Show students how people can be similar and/or different by surveying students and creating class bar graphs about:

- birthday months
- number of people in a family
- eye or hair color
- favorite colors
- favorite foods
- number of siblings

### Discussion Starters:

- What did you notice?
- What was the most/least common answer?

# All About My Family

# My Family Is Special

**1.** Draw a picture of your family.

**2.** My family is special because...

______________________________

______________________________

______________________________

# A Family Postcard

Create a family postcard to show and tell about something your family enjoys doing together.

Front of postcard

Back of postcard

To:

# Rules and Responsibilities: Activities

### Activity Idea: Families Work Together

In a whole-group setting, ask students if they think families are important and to explain their thinking with examples. Then, ask the students to think about special contributions each family member makes to the family. Record the student responses on a chart. Put check marks or tally marks to show repeat answers. Encourage students to think about their own role in their family. What do they contribute? How is it helpful to the family?

Give students a family chart to take home and record how their family works together.

### Extension:

The teacher may wish to talk about how the students and the teacher work together in the classroom.

### Activity Idea: Rules and Responsibilities at Home

Using paper strips, have the students brainstorm different rules that students have at home. List the different rules on a chart and ask the students if they have each rule at their home. Some of the rules that might be stated are: I have a bedtime, I am not allowed to go near the stove without an adult, I need to be polite, I need to tidy up my toys, etc.

### Discussion Starters:

1. Which rules keep you safe at home?

2. Which rules help keep you healthy?

3. Which rules help the members of your family to get along?

4. What do you think would happen if you didn't have any rules at home?

5. What rules would you change? Why?

### Activity Idea: Rules and Responsibilities at School

Have the students use paper strips to brainstorm classroom or school rules. Some rules might include: Walk in the hallways, keep your hands to yourself, be polite, ask permission to go to the bathroom, etc.

### Discussion Starters:

1. Ask the students which rule they feel is the most important.

2. Who do you think should make up the rules in the classroom or at school? Explain your thinking.

3. Which rules help keep you safe?

4. Which rules help you learn?

5. What are your responsibilities at school?

6. What are the responsibilities of the people who work at your school?

### Activity Idea: Rules in Public Places

Do the same as above, but refer to public places.

# Family Members Work Together

Please fill out this chart to help your child develop an understanding of how families function and how various family members contribute. For example: my sister helps feed the baby, my parents cook meals. Encourage your child to think about their own role in your family. What do they contribute? How do they help?

| Family Member | Job or Contribution |
|---|---|
|  |  |
|  |  |
|  |  |
|  |  |
|  |  |

# A Great Rule

**1.**  A rule at _______________________________ is important, because

_______________________________________________________________

**2.**  Make a poster about your rule.

# Healthy Habits: Activity Ideas

## Activity Idea: Having a Healthy Lifestyle

Encourage children to form healthy habits from a young age. In a whole-group setting, introduce the concept of a healthy lifestyle. A healthy lifestyle has four parts: eating healthily, exercising, sleeping enough, and taking time to relax. List the four parts on chart paper and have students brainstorm and list things they can do to support each part.

### Extension:

- Invite guest speakers from various organizations to talk to students about how they can have a healthy lifestyle.

## Activity Idea: The Five Food Groups

Introduce students to the idea that food can be classified into five food groups. Tell them about MyPlate Food Guide, and how there are recommended amounts from each food group that kids should eat each day. Different foods give our bodies important nutrients. Carbohydrates such as potatoes, bread, and cereal give energy. Proteins in meats, fish, nuts, eggs, and some plants help make our bodies grow strong. Vitamins and minerals in fruit, milk products, and vegetables help our bones, teeth, and skin stay healthy. Water helps carry all the other nutrients to different areas in the body.

On chart paper, post the headings of the five food groups: fruits, vegetables, grains, protein, and dairy. Have the students brainstorm food items and record them under the appropriate food group heading.

Encourage students to visit the following website. These games offer students the opportunity to test their food knowledge.

**http://www.nourishinteractive.com/kids/healthy-games**

## Activity Idea: Calories Are Units of Energy

Introduce to students the idea that a calorie is a unit of energy that comes from the food we eat. Some foods, such as sugary treats, have lots of calories. Other foods, such as celery, have very few calories. Reinforce the idea that calories aren't bad for you and that your body needs calories for energy. It is only when you eat too many calories and do not burn enough energy through activity that calories can lead to weight gain.

The recommended range of calories for most school-age children is 1,600 to 2,500 per day. Keep in mind that each person's body burns energy, or calories, at different rates, depending on their size and level of physical activity. Consequently, there is not one fixed number of calories that each child should eat.

### Extension:

- Would you rather have veggies or a cupcake for a snack? Is that a good food choice? Tell why.
- Would you rather eat some chicken for dinner, or a hamburger? Is that a good food choice? Tell why.
- Would you rather have a chocolate bar for breakfast, or cereal? Is that a good food choice? Tell why.
- Would you rather eat at a fast-food restaurant or eat your favorite home-cooked meal? Is that a good food choice? Tell why.

## Activity Idea: Kids' Health Website

The website below is an excellent way for students to learn more about healthy habits. There is an abundant amount of information available in kid-friendly language. There are also many games and other interactive activities where students can find out about: Dealing with Feelings; Staying Healthy; People, Places, and Things That Help Me; and Growing Up.

**http://kidshealth.org/kids/**

# MyPlate Food Guide

## Vegetables
**40% of your plate**

salad 

juice 

## Fruits
**10% of your plate**

## Grains
**30% of your plate**

cereal 

bread 

rice 

pasta 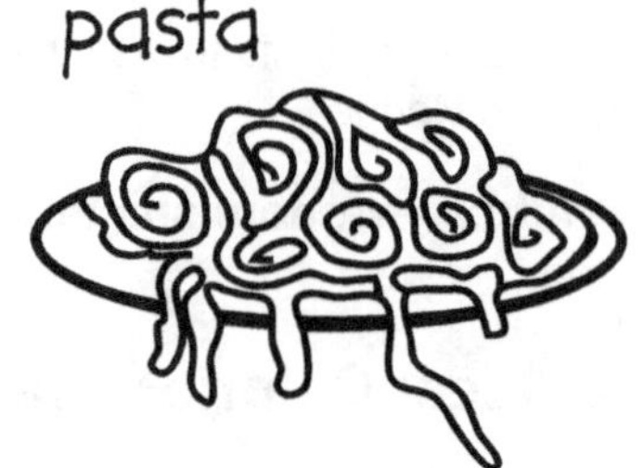

## Dairy
**1 cup of milk, yogurt, or soy milk, 1½ ounces of natural cheese, or 2 ounces of processed cheese**

 milk

cheese 

yogurt 

## Protein
**20% of your plate**

egg 

poultry 

beans

meat 

peanut butter

fish

# Plan a Healthy Eating Day!

List the different kinds of foods and the portion sizes you would eat in a day.

| | | |
|---|---|---|
| 1. | **Breakfast** | |
| 2. | Healthy Snack | |
| 3. | Lunch | |
| 4. | Healthy Snack | |
| 5. | Dinner | |
| 6. | **What are some healthy drink choices?** | |

**How many portions of each food group did you include in your plan?**

Grains: ☐☐☐☐☐☐☐        Fruits: ☐☐☐☐☐☐ ☐☐        Dairy: ☐☐☐☐☐☐☐☐

Vegetables: ☐☐☐☐☐☐ ☐        Protein: ☐☐☐☐☐☐☐

**Explain why you think your eating plan is healthy.**

_______________________________________________________________

_______________________________________________________________

# Healthy or Not Healthy?

Cut and paste the pictures into the correct box. Add some of your own ideas.

# Healthy Food Collage

Cut and paste pictures of healthy food from flyers and magazines to create a collage.

**1.** **Why did you choose some of the foods?**

_______________________________________________

_______________________________________________

_______________________________________________

# Eat Healthy

Create a poster with a message to encourage people to Eat Healthy! Make sure your poster includes a message and a picture.

# Eat Healthy Challenge

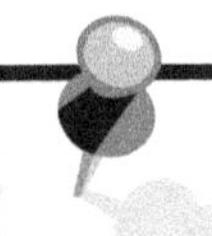 

*Dear Parents and Guardians,*

As part of our class focus on Healthy Habits, we would like families to take part in our Eat Healthy Challenge.

The purpose of the Eat Healthy Challenge is to encourage kids to follow a healthy diet.

Challenge your child to have at least five portions of fruits and vegetables a day. Over the next five days, keep track of the number of fruits and vegetables your child eats.

Every time your child eats a fruit or vegetable, color in a box on the chart. At the end of five days, complete the reflection sheet showing how your child did.

In addition, whole families are welcome to take the challenge!

Your family's participation and support are greatly appreciated!

*Kind Regards,*

_________________________________

# Recording Chart: Eat Healthy Challenge

Can you eat at least five servings of fruit and vegetables a day for five days in a row? Good luck on the Eat Healthy Challenge!

| Day 1 | Day 2 | Day 3 | Day 4 | Day 5 |
|---|---|---|---|---|
|  |  |  |  |  |
|  |  |  |  |  |
|  |  |  |  |  |
|  |  |  |  |  |
|  |  |  |  |  |

1. **How do you think you did? Explain.**

_______________________________________________

_______________________________________________

# Think About It: Eat Healthy Challenge

1. **Do you think you made healthy food choices? Explain your thinking.**

_______________________________________________

_______________________________________________

2. **Who helped to make your food choices?**

_______________________________________________

_______________________________________________

3. **What was the best part about the challenge?**

_______________________________________________

_______________________________________________

4. **What was the hardest part about the challenge?**

_______________________________________________

_______________________________________________

5. **What are your favorite fruits and vegetables?**

_______________________________________________

_______________________________________________

# Student Certificate

How do you feel about completing the challenge? ________________________

________________________________________________________________

# Healthy Teeth

Keep your teeth healthy and strong!
How many of the following things do you do?

| Activity | | |
|---|---|---|
| Visit your dentist regularly | Yes | No |
| Brush your teeth carefully | Yes | No |
| Brush your teeth carefully after every meal | Yes | No |
| Floss your teeth every day | Yes | No |
| Eat healthy foods | Yes | No |

**1.** **Do you think you take care of your teeth? What could you do better? Explain.**

__________________________________________________

__________________________________________________

__________________________________________________

**2.** **Do you like visiting the dentist? Why or why not?**

__________________________________________________

__________________________________________________

Visit this website to learn more about keeping your teeth healthy and strong:
**http://www.mouthhealthykids.org/en**

# Get Enough Sleep

People need sleep to keep healthy, happy, and able to do their best. Sometimes when people don't get enough sleep they feel grumpy and tired. Children ages 5 to 12 need between ten and eleven hours of sleep each night!

**Sleep helps your brain, so you can:**

- Remember what you learn
- Concentrate and be alert
- Think of new ideas
- Solve problems better

**Sleep helps your body, so you can:**

- Stay healthy and be able to fight sickness
- Grow strong

**Here are some sleep tips for a good night's sleep:**

- Make sure your bedroom is cool, dark, and quiet
- Exercise during the day
- Keep a regular bedtime
- Don't drink sodas that have caffeine

**Brain Stretch: Get Enough Sleep!**

1. Why is sleep important?

_______________________________________________

_______________________________________________

_______________________________________________

_______________________________________________

2. How do you feel if you don't get enough sleep? Explain.

_______________________________________________

_______________________________________________

_______________________________________________

_______________________________________________

# Get Enough Sleep

Create a poster with a message to encourage kids to Get Enough Sleep! Make sure your poster includes a message and a picture.

## Get Enough Sleep!

# Healthy Lifestyle Stamp

Create a stamp to encourage people to have a healthy lifestyle.

1. **Write about your stamp:** ___________________________

_______________________________________________

_______________________________________________

# People Who Help Keep You Healthy

How do these people help keep you healthy?

<table>
<tr><td>1.</td><td>Draw a doctor.</td><td>**Explain**</td></tr>
<tr><td>2.</td><td>Draw a family member.</td><td>**Explain**</td></tr>
<tr><td>3.</td><td>Draw a dentist.</td><td>**Explain**</td></tr>
</table>

# Healthy Habits

Explain why each of the following are healthy habits:

# Personal Safety: Activity Ideas

## Activity Idea: Role-Playing

Have students work in pairs or in small groups and act out different safety scenarios to show what they would do. Scenarios might include:

- A stranger approaches you, what do you do?
- Your friend wants to play with matches, what do you do?
- You get lost at the shopping center, what do you do?
- Your friends want you to play a game on the street, what do you do?
- Your house catches fire, what do you do?

## Activity Idea: People Who Keep You Safe

Help students identify people who help keep them safe. These people may include:

- Police Officer
- Firefighter
- Block Parents
- Crossing Guard

Invite any of the above to come and give a class presentation.

## Activity Idea: Safety Tip Poster

Have students create posters to promote safety tips for various situations and places. Topics may include personal safety, cyber safety, safety in public places, or safety tips for when doing certain activities, such as swimming or riding a bicycle. Make sure to go to the website BAM! Body and Mind for an excellent source of safety information in kid-friendly language. Download safety information cards for student use.

**https://www.cdc.gov/bam/index.html**

## Activity Idea: Create a Safety Brochure

Have students create a safety brochure.  Headings for the brochure could include:

- Whom to Call in an Emergency
- People Who Help Keep You Safe
- Public Places: Safety Tips
- Swimming Safety Tips
- Internet Safety Tips

1. Demonstrate for students how to fold a large piece of paper the same way their brochure will be folded.
2. Next, show students how to plan the layout in pencil.

   - Write the heading for each section where you would like it to be in the brochure
   - Leave room underneath each section to write information
   - Leave room for graphics or pictures

3. Students can then write information to fit the headings. This project could be done as a whole-class project, in small groups, or individually.

## Activity Idea: Journal Topics and Discussion Starters

- What might happen if you play with matches or a lighter?
- Why is it an important rule to cross the street only after looking both ways?
- Why should you wear a seat belt in a car?
- What would you do if there were a fire in your home?
- How do you know you can trust someone? By they way they look? By the job they do?
- What would you do if a stranger approached you and asked you to get into their car?
- Why should you never play with electrical outlets?

# Know Your Address and Phone Number

Dear Families,

Use this form to make sure your child knows his or her address and home phone number.

# Staying Safe at Home

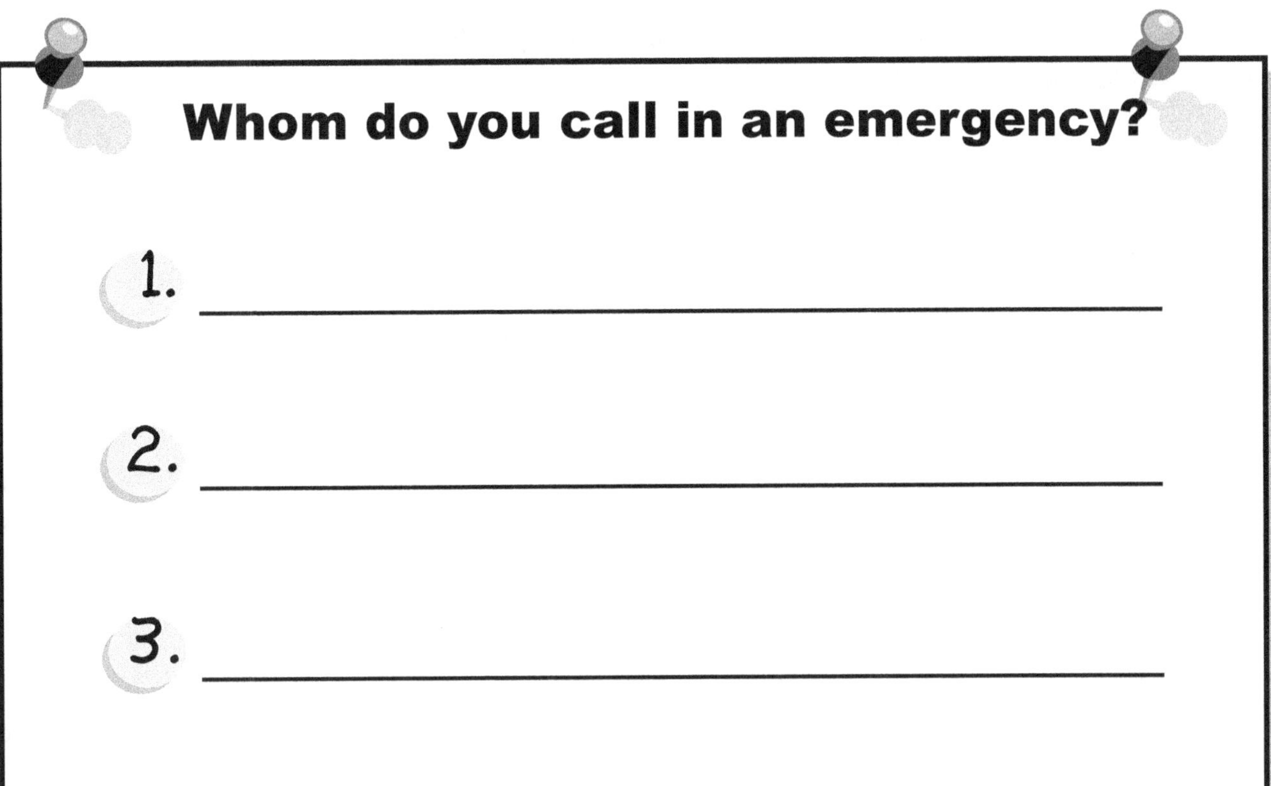

**Whom do you call in an emergency?**

1. _______________________________

2. _______________________________

3. _______________________________

**What are some rules you have at home to keep you safe?**

_______________________________

_______________________________

_______________________________

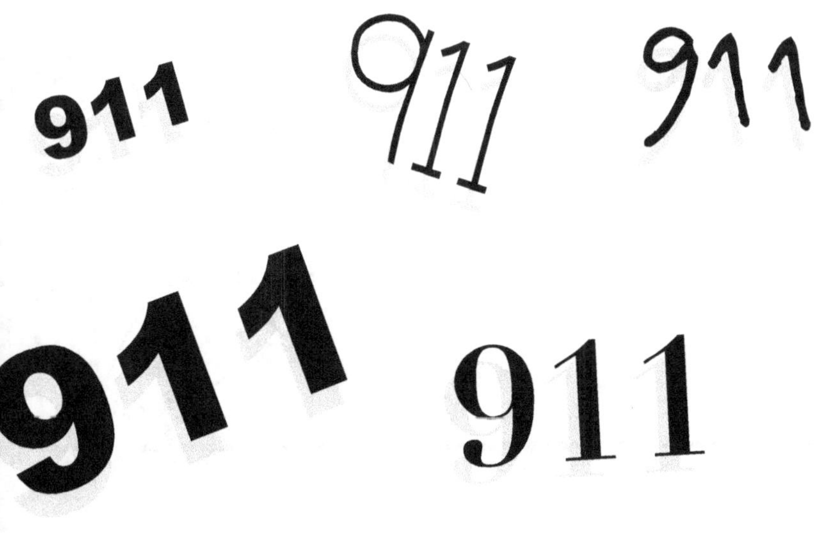

# Staying Safe Tip

Create a poster giving a tip for staying safe. Make sure to include the safety tip and a sentence to explain its importance.

# People Who Help Keep You Safe

How do these people help keep you safe?

**1.** Draw a firefighter.

**Explain**

**2.** Draw a police officer.

**Explain**

**3.** Draw a crossing guard.

**Explain**

# Physical Fitness: Activity Ideas

## Activity Idea: Physical Fitness Survey

As a class, make a list of all of the activities that students might do to be physically active. Answers will vary and might include: skipping rope, riding a bike, dancing, taking a walk, etc. Once the list is complete, survey students to see which activities they have tried, and put tally marks beside the activities.

**Discussion Starters:**

- How often do you do an activity?
- What do you like about it? How does it make you feel?
- Where do you go to do these activities?
- Which activity is on the list that you haven't tried, but would like to?

## Activity Idea: Let's Get Physical!

In a whole-group setting, show students how to check their pulse. Next, have students do a vigorous physical activity, such as jumping jacks, running on the spot, or dancing around the room to upbeat music. Once they have completed the vigorous physical activity, ask students if they feel their heart is beating faster, their lungs are working harder, and/or their bodies feel warm. Explain and reinforce the concept that vigorous physical activity is important to help keep the body healthy and strong.

**Discussion Starters:**

- Ask students to reflect on the physical activity survey and choose which activities would be labeled a vigorous physical activity. Encourage students to explain their thinking.
- Ask students how the vigorous physical activity made them feel.

## Activity Idea: Physical Activity Challenge

Encourage students to keep physically active every day. Ask students to take part in the five-day Physical Activity Challenge. Each day, students will record the physical activities they did, along with the amount of time they did them. Challenge students to do at least 30 minutes of physical activity a day.

As a whole group, brainstorm a list of physical activities they could do. Some examples are:

- playing tag
- playing sports
- dancing
- skipping rope
- playing hopscotch
- swimming
- aerobics
- hiking
- riding a bike
- weight training
- walking/jogging

**Extension:**

- Have students use the word search black line master to create their own word search of physical activities.
- Have students conduct surveys about favorite physical activities.
- Have students create an aerobics routine to an upbeat song.
- Students can take turns leading the class in aerobics activities.
- Have students write a biography of a sports personality. Make sure students include their reasons for choosing that person and what characteristics that person has to have done so well in their chosen sport.

# Recording Chart: Physical Activity Challenge

Congratulations for taking part in the Physical Activity Challenge!

For the next five days, keep track of all the kinds of physical activity you do. Make sure you include things like walking to school, dancing, skipping rope, playing team sports, riding your bike, or playing outside with your friends. Can you do at least 30 minutes of physical activity a day?

| | What kind of physical activity did you do? | How many minutes? |
|---|---|---|
| Day 1 | | |
| Day 2 | | |
| Day 3 | | |
| Day 4 | | |
| Day 5 | | |

# Think About It: Physical Activity Challenge

**1.** How do you think you did?

**2.** What do you enjoy about doing physical activities? Explain.

**3.** What do you not enjoy about doing physical activities? Explain.

**4.** If you could become an expert in two sports, which would you choose?

**5.** Draw a picture of your favorite physical activity.

CONGRATULATIONS!
Name:
YOU HAVE COMPLETED THE PHYSICAL ACTIVITY CHALLENGE

# May I Recommend...

Recommend two things people can do to have a healthy lifestyle. Make sure to explain your thinking!

| I recommend... | Draw a picture. |
| --- | --- |
|  |  |
|  |  |

# Conflict Resolution: Activity Ideas

## Activity Idea: What Is Conflict Resolution?

Introduce the idea of conflict resolution to students. Conflict resolution is a process to help solve problems in a positive way. Each person involved is encouraged to take responsibility for their actions. Clear steps for conflict resolution might include:

- Finding out what the problem is
- Listening without interrupting
- Talking it out
- Coming up with different solutions

Discuss and review the above process with students. Role-play different situations so students can practice walking through the process. Students should be encouraged to try and understand the other person's perspective. The teacher may wish to use situations that are reflected in their class. Encourage students to come up with different solutions so they get in the habit of looking for another solution if the first one does not work. In addition, post the steps for conflict resolution on the board for easy student reference.

## Activity Idea: When People Feel Angry...

Explain to students that sometimes people can feel angry about a situation. People might feel angry because:

- Something is unfair
- Something has been taken away from them
- Something has been broken
- Someone was mean or teased them
- Someone is not sharing
- Someone is in their space

Ask students to remember a time when they felt angry. Have students explain what happened and how they handled the situation. Discuss what would be the best way to handle different situations.

## Activity Idea: Acts of Kindness

Brainstorm with students what it means to be kind. Record their responses on chart paper. Next, go through the student-generated list and have students name the feelings they associate with each act of kindness.

### Discussion Starters:

- What are some ways you can be kind to others?
- How does it feel to be kind? How does it feel to be mean?

Next, have students create coupons to give out to people they would like to perform an act of kindness for. Coupons could be for another student, a family member, neighbor, teacher, etc.

## Activity Idea: Bullying

Help students gain a clear understanding of bullying. Bullying can be described as the act of hurting someone physically or psychologically on purpose. Students should also be made aware that bullies come in all shapes and sizes. Usually someone is bullied repeatedly. Some forms of bullying include:

**Physical:** hitting, punching, tripping, shoving, stealing belongings, locking someone in or out, etc.

**Verbal:** teasing, putting someone down, taunting, making embarrassing remarks, etc.

**Relational:** excluding someone from a group, spreading rumors, ignoring someone, ostracizing someone, etc.

It is hoped that if students can understand what a person feels like when bullied, students will develop empathy and help stop bullying.

# Conflict Scenario Cards: What Would You Do?

### Conflict Scenario Card:

## What would you do?

The teacher has told you to line up for recess. Someone in the class pushes their way in front of you instead of going to the end of the line.

### Conflict Scenario Card:

## What would you do?

Someone in the class has taken your materials without your permission.

### Conflict Scenario Card:

## What would you do?

You are building a structure using construction materials and someone comes and knocks it down on purpose.

### Conflict Scenario Card:

## What would you do?

You and your friends are playing with a ball at recess. Another kid comes along and takes the ball away.

### Conflict Scenario Card:

## What would you do?

You and your best friend get into an argument. Your best friend does not want to play with you anymore.

### Conflict Scenario Card:

## What would you do?

You are trying to do your work at your desk and the same person keeps bothering you.

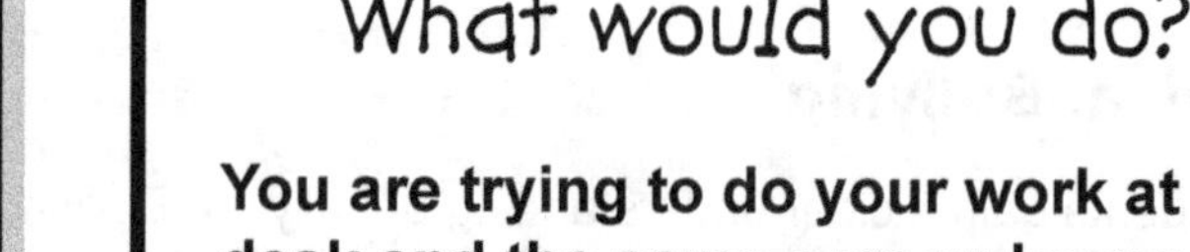

Let's solve the problem!

Step 1

What is
the
problem?

Step 2

Listen without interrupting.

Step 3

Talk
it
out.

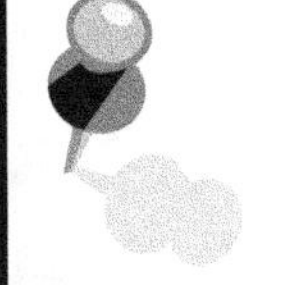

# Step 4

# Come up with a solution.

# Step 5

# Remember to put yourself in the other person's shoes.

# Acts of Kindness

Acts of kindness let people know that you care about them. Color the boxes green that are examples of acts of kindness.

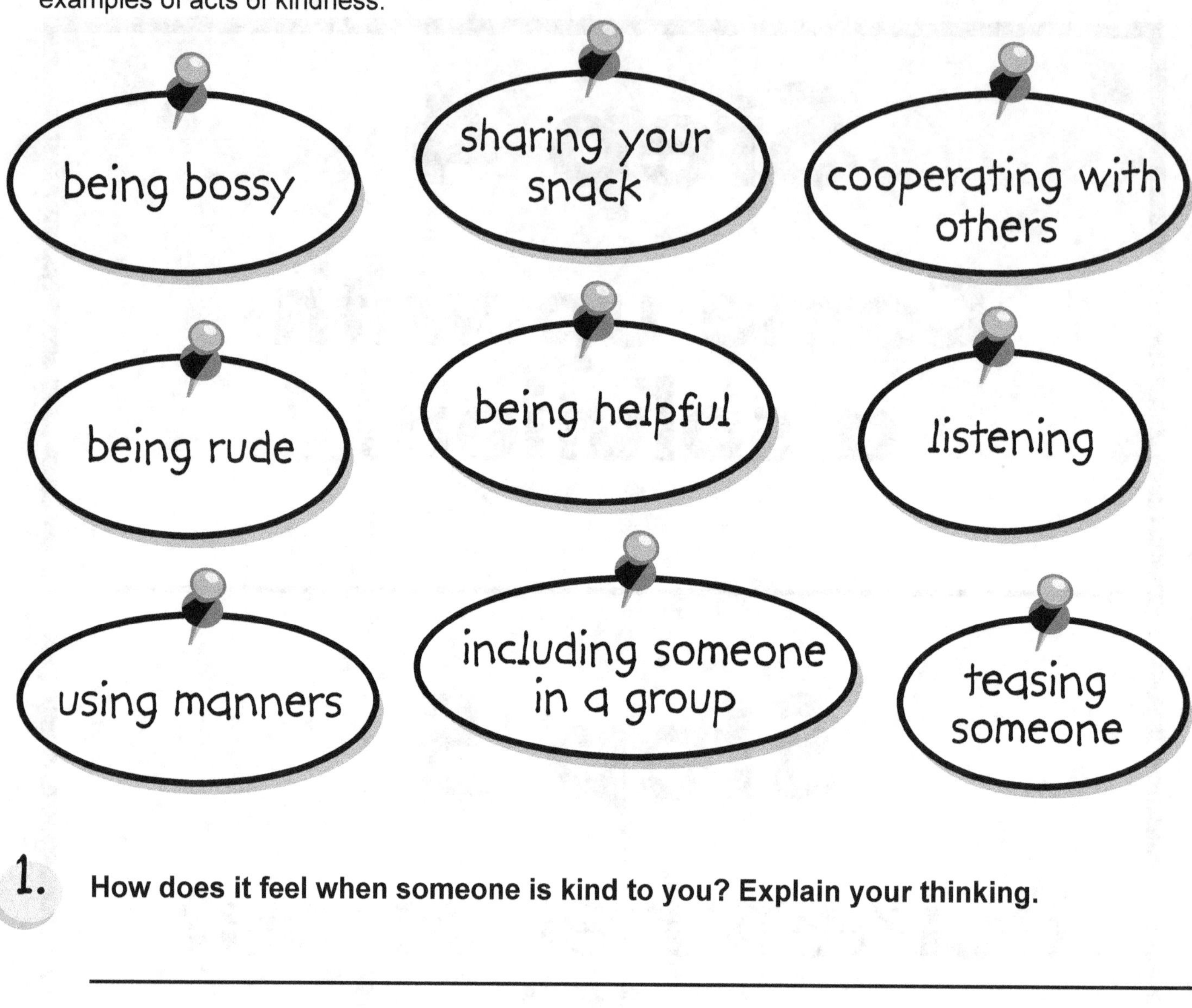


1. How does it feel when someone is kind to you? Explain your thinking.

_______________________________________________

_______________________________________________

2. How does it feel when you are kind to someone? Explain your thinking.

_______________________________________________

_______________________________________________

# Bullying: What Should You Do?

**1.** How do you think a person being bullied feels?

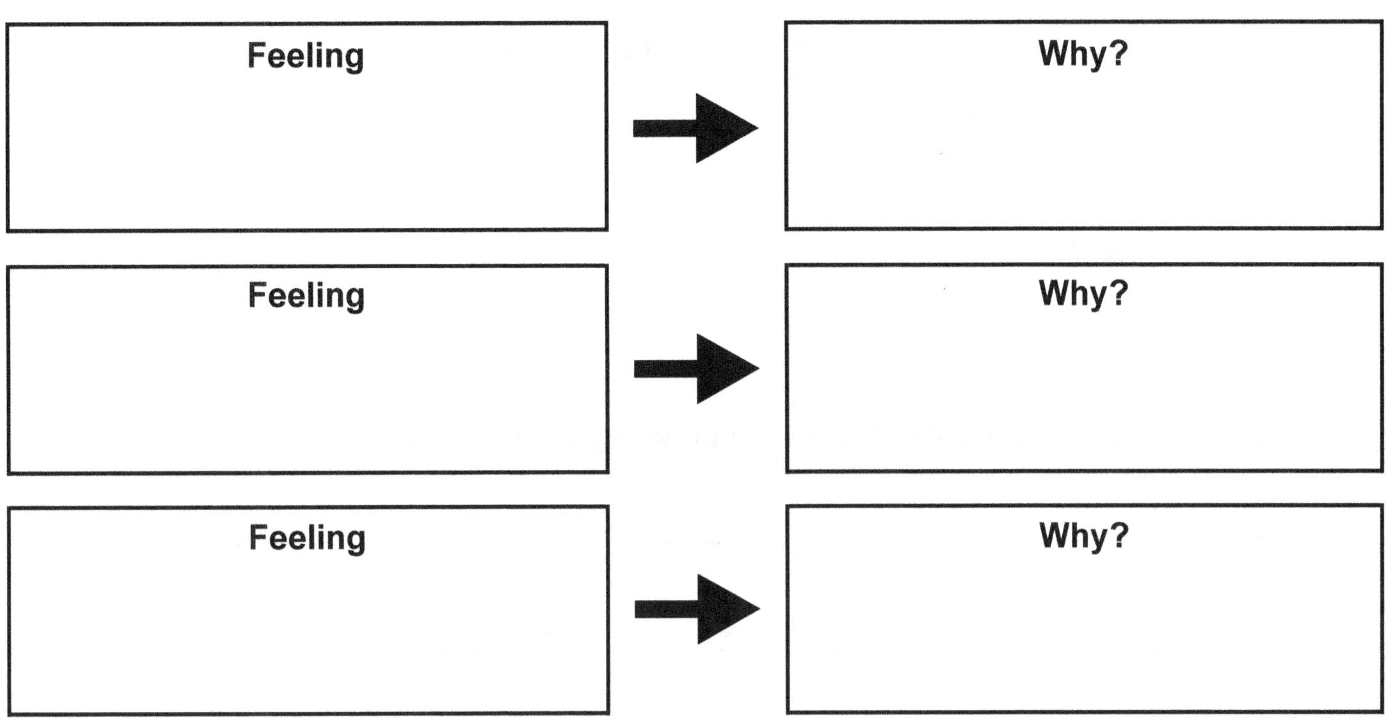



**2.** Circle in **green** the things you should do when bullied.
Circle in **red** the things you should not do when bullied.

# Stop Bullying!

**What is bullying?**

Bullying is when someone mistreats someone on purpose, as in:

- calling someone names or putting them down
- using physical violence
- ignoring or excluding
- spreading rumors

**1.** **What are three things a person who is being bullied can do?**

a. _______________________________________________

b. _______________________________________________

c. _______________________________________________

**2.** **What are three things you can do if you see someone else being bullied?**

a. _______________________________________________

b. _______________________________________________

c. _______________________________________________

# Problem Report

## Problem Report

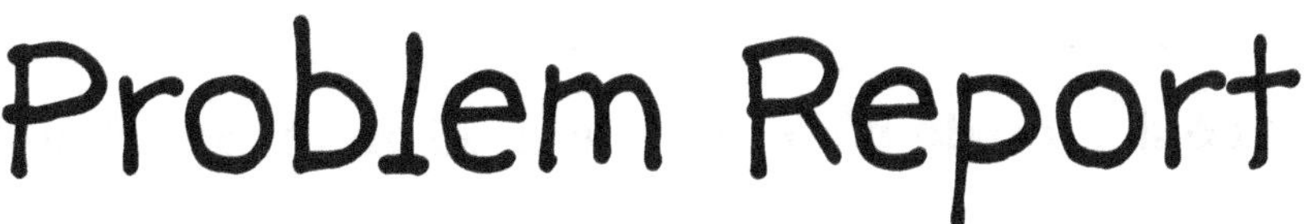

a. What happened? ______________________________

______________________________

b. Has this ever happened to you before? YES NO

c. What did you do? ______________________________

______________________________

d. If this happens again, I should:

- Tell the person to stop
- Go to a safe place
- Tell a teacher

e. Other ______________________________

______________________________

# Stop Bullying! Journal Topics

1. Have you ever been bullied?

2. What could you do if you feel worried about being bullied?

3. Why might someone feel afraid to tell the teacher if they are being bullied?

4. When should you tell a teacher or another adult?

5. Why do people who bully want to keep it a secret?

6. Which type of bullying do you think is the worst? Explain.

7. How do you think someone feels when they are bullied?

8. Have you ever bullied anyone? Why did you do it?

9. What can you do if you see bullying happening?

10. Is it okay to bully someone because you feel angry?

# A Letter of Advice

**Choose:**

- Write a letter of advice to someone who is being bullied.
- Write a letter of advice to someone who is being a bully.

*Dear* _________________________________ ,

_______________________________________

_______________________________________

_______________________________________

_______________________________________

_______________________________________

_______________________________________

_______________________________________

_______________________________________

_______________________________________

_______________________________________

_______________________________________

_______________________________________

*Your friend,*

_______________________________________

# What I Think I Know and What I Wonder About.

Write or draw in the space below.

# Reporting Ideas

## Non-Fiction Reports

Encourage students to read informational text and to recall in their own words what they have read. Provide a theme-related space or table and subject-related materials and artifacts such as books, tapes, posters, magazines, etc.

Have students explore the different sections usually found in a non-fiction book:

1. Title Page: The book title and the author's name

2. Table of Contents: The title of each chapter, what page it starts on, and where you can find specific information

3. Glossary: The meaning of special words used in the book

4. Index: The ABC list of specific topics you can find in the book

Next, discuss the criteria of a good research project. They should include:

- A presentation board or other medium

- Proper grammar and punctuation, for example, capitals and periods

- Print size that can be read from far away

- Neat coloring and detailed drawings

## Oral Reports

Encourage students to talk about what they have learned and to make a presentation to the class. Here are tips to discuss with students:

- Use your best voice, speak slowly, and make sure your voice is loud so everyone can hear

- Look at your audience and try not to sway

- Introduce your topic in an interesting way, for instance, by using a riddle or a question

- Choose the most important information to tell

- Point to pictures, a model, or a diorama as you present

# A Web About...

Fill in the circles below.

# A T-chart About...

Fill in the chart below.

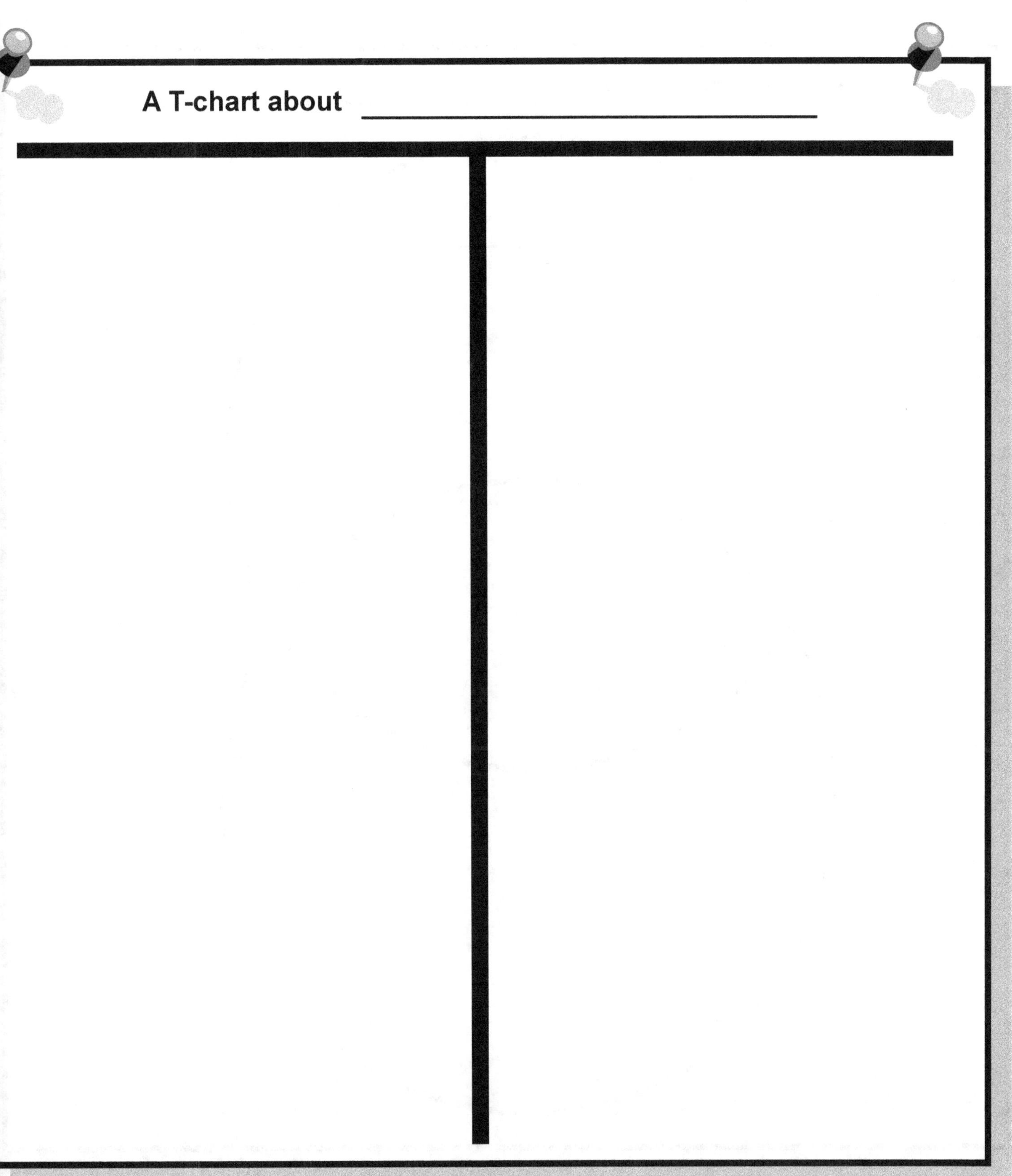

# A Venn Diagram About...

Fill in the diagram below.

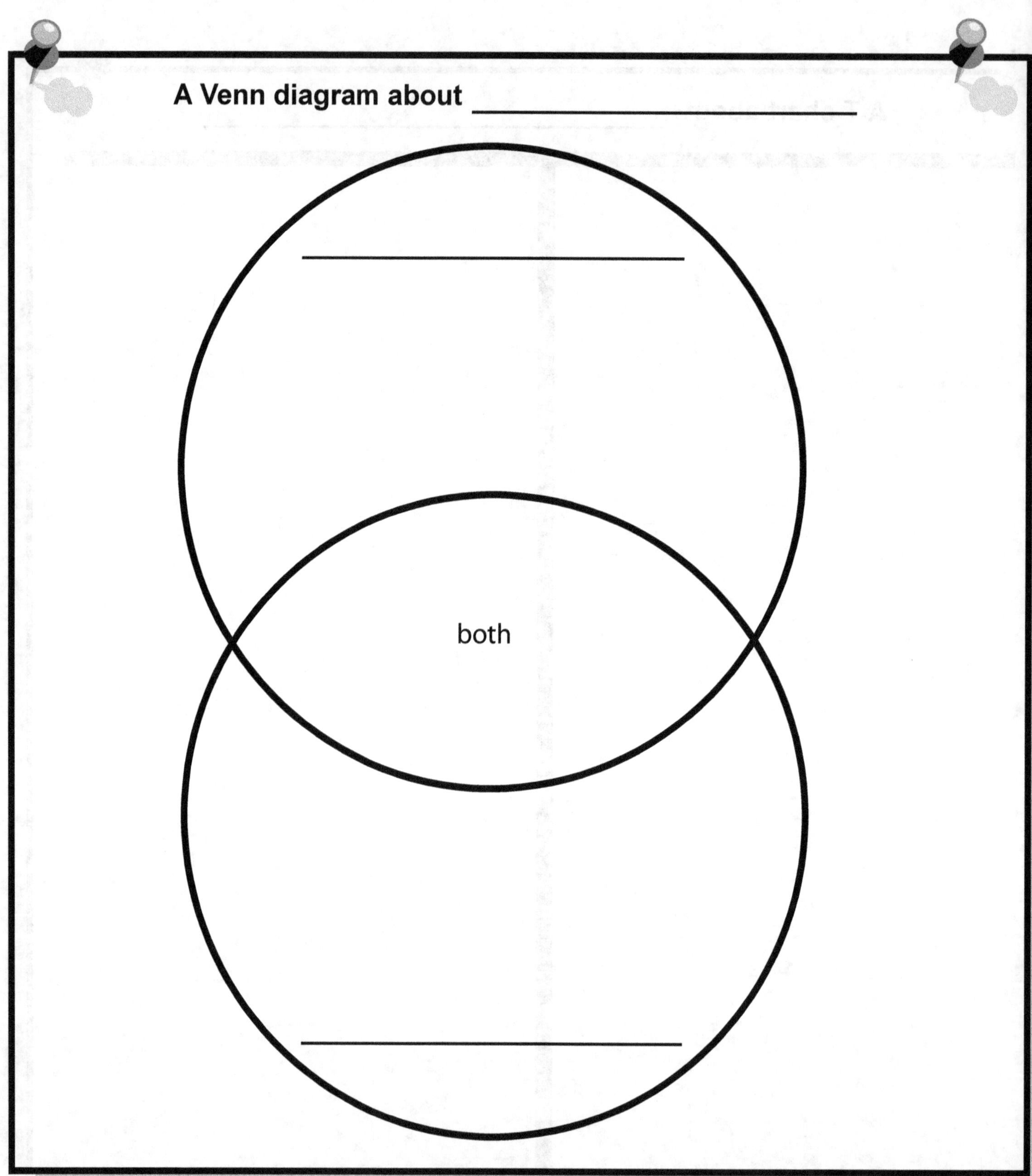

# Survey Outline

1. What is the question? _______________________________________

2. How many people are you going to ask? _______________________

| Answer Choices | Tally Marks |
| --- | --- |
|  |  |
|  |  |
|  |  |
|  |  |
|  |  |
|  |  |
|  |  |

3. Once you have completed your survey, create a bar graph to show the information.

# Conduct a Survey

**1.** This is a graph about ________________________

**2.** Survey title ________________________

**3.** I found out that...

________________________

________________________

________________________

# Student Rubric

| Level | Student Participation Descriptor |
| --- | --- |
| Level 4 | Student consistently contributes to class discussions and activities by offering ideas and asking questions. |
| Level 3 | Student usually contributes to class discussions and activities by offering ideas and asking questions. |
| Level 2 | Student sometimes contributes to class discussions and activities by offering ideas and asking questions. |
| Level 1 | Student rarely contributes to class discussions or activities by offering ideas or asking questions. |

| Level | Understanding of Concepts Descriptor |
| --- | --- |
| Level 4 | Student shows a thorough understanding of all or almost all concepts and consistently gives appropriate and complete explanations independently. No teacher support is needed. |
| Level 3 | Student shows a good understanding of most concepts and usually gives complete or nearly complete explanations. Infrequent teacher support is needed. |
| Level 2 | Student shows a satisfactory understanding of most concepts and sometimes gives appropriate, but incomplete, explanations. Teacher support is sometimes needed. |
| Level 1 | Student shows little understanding of concepts and rarely gives complete explanations. Intensive teacher support is needed. |

| Level | Communication of Concepts Descriptor |
| --- | --- |
| Level 4 | Student consistently communicates with clarity and precision in written and oral work. Student consistently uses appropriate terminology and vocabulary. |
| Level 3 | Student usually communicates with clarity and precision in written and oral work. Student usually uses appropriate terminology and vocabulary. |
| Level 2 | Student sometimes communicates with clarity and precision in written and oral work. Student sometimes uses appropriate terminology and vocabulary. |
| Level 1 | Student rarely communicates with clarity or precision in written or oral work. |

# Class Evaluation List

Fill in the following:

| Student Name | Class Participation | Understanding of Concepts | Communication of Concepts | Overall Evaluation |
| --- | --- | --- | --- | --- |
|  |  |  |  |  |
|  |  |  |  |  |
|  |  |  |  |  |
|  |  |  |  |  |
|  |  |  |  |  |
|  |  |  |  |  |
|  |  |  |  |  |
|  |  |  |  |  |
|  |  |  |  |  |
|  |  |  |  |  |
|  |  |  |  |  |
|  |  |  |  |  |
|  |  |  |  |  |

# Physical Activity Rubric

| | Level 1 | Level 2 | Level 3 | Level 4 |
|---|---|---|---|---|
| **Understanding of Physical Activity Concepts** | Student demonstrates a limited understanding of concepts. | Student demonstrates a satisfactory understanding of concepts. | Student demonstrates a complete understanding of concepts. | Student demonstrates a thorough understanding of concepts. |
| **Application of Skills Taught** | Student applies few of the required skills. | Student applies some of the required skills. | Student applies most of the required skills. | Student applies almost all of the required skills. |
| **Participation** | Constant teacher encouragement is needed. | Some teacher encouragement is needed. | Little teacher encouragement is needed. | Student almost always participates without teacher encouragement. |
| **Sportsmanship** | Student needs encouragement to be a team player. | Student will occasionally share, help, and encourage others. | Student will usually share, help, and encourage others. | Student acts as a team leader. Student will consistently share, help, and encourage others. |
| **Safety** | Student requires constant reminders regarding safety or the safe use of equipment and facilities. | Student requires occasional reminders regarding safety or the safe use of equipment and facilities. | Student requires few reminders regarding safety or the safe use of equipment and facilities. | Student requires almost no reminders regarding safety or the safe use of equipment and facilities. |

# Thinking About My Work...

**Thinking About My Work**

1. I am proud of:

_______________________________________________

2. I want to learn more about:

_______________________________________________

3. I need to work on:

_______________________________________________

4. I will do better by:

_______________________________________________

**Thinking About My Work**

1. I am proud of:

_______________________________________________

2. I want to learn more about:

_______________________________________________

3. I need to work on:

_______________________________________________

4. I will do better by:

_______________________________________________

# Useful Health Websites

**1.** All About Kids' Health
**http://kidshealth.org/en/kids/**

**2.** Safe Kids Worldwide
**https://www.safekids.org/united-states-0**

**3.** An Anti-Bullying Site
**https://www.stopbullying.gov/**

**4.** Stay Alert …Stay Safe
**http://kidshealth.org/en/kids/watch/**

**5.** The American Lung Association
**http://www.lung.org/**

**6.** The American Dental Association
**http://www.mouthhealthykids.org/en**

**7.** Kids Environment, Kids Health
**https://kids.niehs.nih.gov/**

**8.** MyPlate Food Guide
**http://kidshealth.org/en/kids/pyramid.html**

**9.** Websites for Kids and Teens
**https://www.cdc.gov/family/kidsites/index.htm**

**10.** Fire Safety Tips for Kids
**http://www.firesafetyforkids.org/fire-safety-rules.html**

# CONGRATULATIONS!

Name: _______________________